BRING YOUR WORTH

LEVEL UP YOUR CREATIVE POWER, VALUE & SERVICE TO THE WORLD

Damon Brown
www.DamonBrown.net
JoinDamon.me

TWITTER/INSTAGRAM: *@BROWNDAMON*
CONSULTING & SPEAKING REQUESTS:
DAMON@DAMONBROWN.NET

PUBLISHED BY:
Damon Brown

Bring Your Worth
1st Edition
Copyright 2019 by Damon Brown
Edited by Jeanette Hurt
Cover designed by The Bec Effect
Cover photo by Alex Goetz

All rights reserved. Without limiting the rights under copyright reserved above, no part of this publication may be reproduced, stored in or introduced into a retrieval system, or transmitted, in any form, or by any means (electronic, mechanical, photocopying, recording, or otherwise) without the prior written permission of both the copyright owner and the above publisher of the book.

The author acknowledges the trademarked status and trademark owners of various products referenced in this work, which have been used without permission. The publication/use of these trademarks is not authorized, associated with, or sponsored by the trademark owners.

To Papaya

"You must be selfish enough to be in alignments with your true self before you have anything to give."

*Esther & Jerry Hicks,
The Vortex*

Reading

Selected Books By The Author

How to Bring Your Worth   I

I. Bring Your Worth   1

II. Get Your Worth   19

III. Share Your Worth   45

Conclusion   71

Let's Connect!   83

Available Keynote Talks   85

Significant References   89

Acknowledgements   93

About the Author   95

SELECTED BOOKS BY THE AUTHOR

THE ULTIMATE BITE-SIZED ENTREPRENEUR:

76 WAYS TO BOOST TIME, PRODUCTIVITY & FOCUS ON YOUR BIG IDEA

THE PASSIVE WRITER:

5 STEPS TO EARNING MONEY IN YOUR SLEEP

(W/ JEANETTE HURT)

OUR VIRTUAL SHADOW:

WHY WE ARE OBSESSED WITH DOCUMENTING OUR LIVES ONLINE

PORN & PONG:

HOW GRAND THEFT AUTO, TOMB RAIDER AND OTHER SEXY GAMES CHANGED OUR CULTURE

How to Bring Your Worth

Why does the market not value my true worth?

Why does my bank account not reflect my true worth?

Why does the world not understand my true worth?

The more unique your voice in the world, the more difficult it may be to see your true worth in the marketplace, in your bank account, and in the world. If you don't feel like you are receiving what you deserve, then perhaps it is not a reflection of the world, but a reflection of how you truly feel about your own worth.

You have to bring your worth to make your mark on the world.

Did you ever try to believe that things are how they are supposed to be? The chaos, the pain, and the challenges in your life are supposed to be there.

It hurts. Open up to that possibility for a moment, though, and you begin twisting the things in your world from different angles. Life isn't a flat board, but more like a Rubix Cube, and the more sides you view, the more of the puzzle you see, and creating a bigger discussion, and, for you, a bigger life. But, again, that requires accepting where you are. That's the hard part.

Unfortunately, you cannot truly make an impact on the world until you believe you are where you are supposed to be. Resenting your station only makes you misunderstand your gifts, if you see them at all. Fighting the life you have now only tires you out and distracts you from the real fight to become your truest self. Bitterness costs you opportunities. This presents a real, yet silent, problem.

For a period of time, my toddler would just say "No" to everything offered to him. My partner and I would eventually stare at him with puzzled expressions, and he would become increasingly frustrated. He made it clear to us of what he didn't want, but he wouldn't actually say what he *did* want. We couldn't help him. It might sound ridiculous, especially if you've never raised a toddler, but we do the exact same thing every day. We get tired of shitty-paying clients, we loathe that organizations hold all the power, we feel downright mad that the world doesn't recognize our genius. But what are we bringing to the situation?

You have to bring your worth to the table to get your worth from your partnerships and then serve your worth to the world. Step into your role, and the world embraces you on that level. It is made just for you. It cannot be taken away. You cannot be replaced. It means only you possess the puzzle piece fitting uniquely, snugly, perfectly into that role. You cannot be replaced, but you also do not have a back-up. There is no understudy for you.

It is a three-legged stool: Your worth to the marketplace, your worth to the bank account, and your worth to the world. Bring two of these to the table and you may keep going for a little bit, but your career won't persevere. Bring only one to the table, and you're not going to make it – you'll topple before you even sit down.

Base your worth only on what the market desires, then you're following the current trends – which is what everyone else is doing. You're on a race to the bottom, as Seth Godin says, making your products and services cheaper than the competition, as that's the only bargaining tool you'll have to offer. You won't be original. Worse, since you're eager to hop onto the next trend, your community will feel abandoned, and in time, they likely will stop following you because they know you will eventually leave them.

Base your worth only on what the bank account needs, then you're putting getting paid over serving your community. One of two things, and likely both, will almost certainly happen: Either you'll get sloppy at your work because you're prioritizing the money, or your customers will recognize that you're just in it for the money. They will recognize you just don't really care about them. People are always more perceptive than we think.

Base your worth only on what the world needs, then congratulations: You're a starving artist. This is perhaps the saddest outcome, as there is no relationship between the quality of your work and you actually getting paid for your work. They are not inversely proportional. And if there were any inkling of an argument, it would be for the reverse. I've been a starving artist, and if you have been as well, then you know there is a significant amount of brain power dedicated to just figuring out your next meal.

Personally, I serve everyone better on a full stomach.

If *The Bite-Sized Entrepreneur* helped you with its tactics to fulfill your creative destiny, then *Bring Your Worth*, its spiritual successor, will aid you in living a more authentic (and valued) life.

Bring Your Worth is the live album as much as *The Bite-Sized Entrepeneur* series was the studio sessions. Inspired by my Create Your Worth keynotes, my TED Talks, and the many worldwide conversations I've had with you, my readers and listeners, this book breaks down the three legs you need to bring your full innovative value, power, and service to the world. You're not trying to create your worth, find your worth, or build your worth. You just need bring the strength you already have.

You need to recognize it first, though. Consider this your first step.

-Damon

December 2018

I
BRING YOUR WORTH
EVERYTHING IS A PARTNERSHIP

"The artist is afraid of finding out who she is. This fear, I suspect, is more about finding we are greater than we think than discovering that we're lesser.

What if, God help us, we actually have talent? What if we truly do possess a gift?

What will we do then?"

Steven Pressfield,
The Artist's Journey

There's confusion to valuing our own worth. No, it isn't just a job. The sensitives got it right: Your work isn't just an exchange of goods for services. It is the representation of yourself to the world. Aside from neighbors, friends, and loved ones, no one knows you beyond what you put out into the world and, more importantly, what impact you leave behind after you go. The demand for your stuff reflects what you are contributing to the conversation and how much you are committing to your unique perspective. It doesn't make sense to go after something just because it is the new hot thing. The trouble with trends is that other people spot them, too, with the same intention of riding the wave. Everyone else recognizes what is a hot thing, and, unless that hot thing matches your voice, which, if you are lucky, happens once or twice within a lifetime, then you strip away any original proposition you have.

When the trend does match your unique intention, though, then you can drive the market. The goal, then, is staying committed to what you know is important. Not think, but know. It is what Brene Brown means when she says "Braving the wilderness." It is lonely, and it has to be, because being your original self means having no duplicate. The wilderness can be strictly psychological, watching the rejection letters pour in day after day for your ideal project and having the wherewithal to keep going, or it could be financial, pouring your hard-earned pay gained from another, less exciting, path into something you know is your next calling.

Most of all, this knowledge stays silent. It may even be painfully quiet. And, no matter how much you shout, no one will be able to understand you, as if you are speaking Greek on the Roman Isles. This is how it should be. Hearing the thumbs up, the nod, or the go-ahead from anyone is a false positive, particularly from people in control of the market. The voice you begin hearing becomes theirs, not your own, and it is painfully easy to catch amnesia and start forging a path for them instead of a path for yourself. It can be a cruel fate. I've seen it: Brilliant, driven creators, machete in hand swatting through the proverbial Amazon to the sound of their calling, and, in a glimmer, they are just as passionately going in another direction, instead of listening to a gatekeeper's faint promise of security, fame, or money. I know I have succumbed to that siren call myself.

Know this: Gatekeepers themselves don't have security. Gatekeepers don't have the power anymore. They are our partners, your partners, as they should have been all along. The insight garnered from so-called gatekeepers is inversely proportional to the power of technology, which means the vision of, say, a publishing house in the 1960's would have compared to a new author would be much, much further than the same house would have today. We are reaching an inflection point where things are so inversely proportional, creators have a greater vision than those up on high. We are the ones on the front lines. We are the ones connecting with our audiences. We are the ones with the social media followings, the DIY opportunities, and the ability to continually iterate our ideas based on instant feedback. We don't need them. They need us.

‧₃₈₀‧

Alarcity is today's default setting. Entrepreneur Jason Fried reads the news in a newspaper once a day, saying it is the perfect delivery vehicle, as the things that are most important are curated and mentioned and stick around for the following day. It avoids the hyperbole of things seeming important at the moment, and everything can't be important at the moment, for, at that point, then nothing can truly be important at that moment. It is why we suddenly regain balance when we are with very young people, or with kind animals, as they truly are of the moment, not of the overstimulated moment, but of the hyperaware moment. All that matters is now. It is instinctual for them, as they haven't learned to see otherwise, to be concerned with tomorrow and to regret what was done yesterday like an infinity loop. Therapist Esther Perel's family and other European Jews survived World War II, yet Perel says most every individual was either disillusioned for the rest of their lives, which she calls "Joining the walking dead", or focused on making and enjoying every day to the fullest. They had to choose. It is why New Yorkers found clarity in the weeks following 9/11. Traumatic events propel us into hyperawareness. They remind us that we have to choose every day – because that choice was almost taken away from us.

You never know what is at stake. It is more than "Today's intern could become your manager in the future." It is of your intention. The small act magnifies, and how you do one thing is how you do everything. From the universe, sure, you are spiritually showing that you can handle something bigger. That's not the point. The point is the muscle memory, the knee jerk reaction you train yourself to have in the situation when the risk was more minimal. Archilochus said in moments of trouble, we don't rise to the level of our expectations, but we fall to the level of our training.

Picture scaffolding, but instead of from the inside out, picture it going from the outside in. It is our bones, our literal integrity, which difficult times test and fortify. Without challenging ourselves, we do not know if the values we created are really what we believe. The universe, which really means *you*, since you are one with the world, does not create struggle to punish you, but to reconfirm what you actually believe. The confidence to know what you believe isn't complete until you are given ample opportunity to disregard it.

The advocates will come. But first, you need to start.

You want your purpose to be as transparent as a drop of water: Only take a sip, and you are completely understood. You don't need anything deep or heavy, any dramatic pronouncements. Marcus Aurelius said that your truth should be clear as soon as you step into a room, like a smelly goat. That strength is undeniable by the many, even by your detractors, and it is unattainable by the masses, even by the envious. It is pure and unyielding. Once you uncover it, then it can no longer remain buried. This is a gift and a curse, as you cannot unknow it, either, and you will have to do something with it for the rest of your life. Other people will recognize it, too, and those who care about you will dog you to fulfill it, while even those who just met you will know when you are in alignment with it. They will see it in your eyes. Do you ever look at someone and know they are living their truth? It could be ugly, it could be disagreeable, but it always means something higher than just muddling through life. They light up. It is undeniable. It is understood without saying a word.

⊂₃⊃

Words exist, but putting them in a certain order, in a particular cadence, changes the culture. Only a few musical notes exist, and yet, in the right hands – your hands – they number plenty to make a dent in the universe. Your work has value. The rub is that your work may not be tangible. That is, the world at large doesn't see your tangible work. A financial broker makes money moving money around, putting her in the same capacity as a three-card Monty hustler on the boardwalk. And yet, becoming a CPA may be more celebrated than becoming a poet because the path is clear. It is safe.

Get closer to your creative truth, though, and you'll get further from safety. You were never meant to leave the world the same way as you came into it. You know it. That's why it hurts. Taking a leap rarely hurts, even when you fail. The pain arrives from the separation between who you are being and who you really are. Bonding with your truth is inversely proportional to clinging to your safety.

This value question isn't just yours, though, but everyone else's, too. Being closer to your truth makes you shine, and when others connect with you, they recognize their own gap between being and self. They feel your power. It triggers their own choices between safety and truth. They have to raise their own awareness, stop interacting with you anymore, or remind you of the futility of your path. Or they could do all three. Responses always reflect other people's view of their worth. Always. This is why bringing your worth is essential to any relationship, whether invoicing a client or pitching an idea or launching a service or explaining what you do at a cocktail party. Every interaction is a building block, and you're either adding or subtracting to this foundation to get closer to your true self and, therefore, your true worth. I have done lateral moves and even some steps back, and they serve as reminders of what I am not. As many wise people have said, setbacks are not failures, but information: Data on what you are not, figures showing your real path, live feedback on your pain points. The times when you undervalue yourself - and actually get what you asked for! - are just as valuable as the times you are able to reflect your true worth. It all depends on what you do with the insight.

☙

Your longing for success creates enough fuel to draw in the right clients, build the best career, and create a higher opportunity for you. Drop the dialogue on crushing the competition, because when you are in tune with your intention, then there is no competition. There doesn't need to be concerns about the timeline, as things jump into place when they line up, not when you hit a time-based milestone. And frustration over your current situation should be acknowledged, but only as a barometer for what you don't want in the future, as your disdain for today will keep you focused only on what you lack now rather than what you desire tomorrow. Be as clear and as transparent and as honest as possible about what you want, regardless of your current moment, as the more visionary you become with your future, the more you will, knowingly and unknowingly, start to build systems to make it real.

One of the best ways to make your best work for the world is to create without the intention of shipping, launching, or selling. It doesn't mean working for free. It means working without expectations. Our biggest ideas are as fragile as a Parisian croissant, and the pressure of projected success can make them crumble before we even have the opportunity to see what they will become. They are too abstract to handle the stress test. It is why we should create pilots, just simple, minimal viable products that can get our ideas out. It is why we should do side hustles, fun pursuits we do outside of our 9-to-5 during, as entrepreneur Chase Jarvis says, our 5-to-9. It is why we should build support networks, so we know there are other people trying to make something out of nothing.

All these solutions have one thing in common: You are sharing and, then, listening. Pilots give you feedback from the people you want to serve, side hustles give you feedback from the financial realities of your pursuit, and networks give you feedback from your peers. Our biggest problems come when we are using our will rather than our intuition or, simply, our ears.

Do not get a win and attribute it to just your will, as if our anger or our frustration bended the universe to our desires. More often, though, we have our major breakthroughs, our quantum leaps, and our milestone moments when we are on our knees. The darkness before the dawn, the opening right in the nick of time, and so on, are cliches for a reason. It's high drama, sure, and gives us survivors a story to tell. But it also reflects that moment when we are ready to give up, because when we are ready to give up, we are the most open to aligning rather than maligning the future.

II
GET YOUR WORTH
DON'T WAIT FOR PERMISSION

"But this payment goes well beyond my generosity," the monk responded.

"Don't say that again," said The Alchemist. "Life may be listening, and give you less next time."

> *Paulo Coehlo,*
> *The Alchemist*

We are magicians. Our best work is creating something out of nothing. It is all binary. It doesn't matter if you are a writer, rearranging the same words that have existed well before your grandmother's grandmother was born, or an architect, turning scribbles written down from your mind's eye into a physical space, or a priest, literally calling upon the heavens which no living man has set foot in. Our best work is always invisible, as even the most physical acts have an alchemy that happens behind the scenes, a chemical reaction that happens within you, transforming what once was into what was never before. This is yours and yours alone. And this is yours to keep.

The challenge happens when we measure our work based on society standards instead of actual impact. For instance, a mason would be one of the most revered, well-paid people in our community in the 19th century, fashioning the bricks building our homes, kilning the shoes carrying the horses we ride, and finishing the weapons protecting our lives from harm. Today, masons are respected, but they aren't deemed as important to the general public. They are not as valued. Computer-aided design, smart cars, and equally smart weapons have taken over their role.

Now, take this idea to the small scale. Bring this paradigm to what you believe in. Pursuing something because it's the hot thing today makes sense in the short term. You aren't terribly interested, and you may even hate it, but you know that's what sells, and that's what the market seems to demand. Worse, you may get your first paycheck for it, and you can mistake something as a calling because someone is willing to pay you for it. The problem is two fold. First, if you're jumping on the bandwagon, then other people will be or, more likely, already are getting into that same competitive space. That's the very definition of bandwagon. You are almost certainly going to lose. Second, and more importantly, you are creating something that is unsustainable both externally and internally. You are doing something that you don't really care about and you are doing something that, almost inevitably, the market will stop monetarily valuing. You get the worst of both worlds.

It is wiser to trust the market cycles to do just that: cycle. Staying steadfast to your particular thing actually builds more security than hopping from trend to trend, as you build momentum, you build reputation, and you build community based on that very thing you care most about. People who give a shit about that thing will recognize your craftsmanship, or your dedication, or your commitment, and will reward you with their attention. Attention, not money, is the most powerful currency one can give you, as money is renewable, but time is not. And once the sun shines on your particular craft, then you will rise like cream to the top, as much as we're obsessed with science, technology, engineering, and mathematics (STEM) today, just as we were focused on web developers at the turn of the millennium, and on

Wall Street whiz kids two decades before that. The biggest influencers of every era blaze brightly based on those proverbial 10,000 hours of study, and that doesn't happen, and can't happen, because the market is interested in what they care about. They have to proceed well before the market approves what they value. They cannot wait for the world's seal of approval.

Unmistakable author Srinivas Rao compares business to surfing. When you are looking for a wave to ride, you don't go after the beautiful, fully-formed ones. They are in the distance. Remember, you have to recognize the opportunity, direct your board, and create momentum to head there. By the time you get there, the wave will crash, likely on top of you. If you see the white caps, though, where new waves are forming, then you start heading in that direction based on instinct. It isn't obvious. It is likely only seen by you, based on your own viewpoint, experience, and eyesight. The wave is yours and yours alone, and, as it crests, you ride it as if you own it, because you do. Others may view you as an overnight success, as a visionary, or as a lucky bastard. You just got quiet enough to pay attention to your own voice.

And no matter how they feel, they will happily pay you what your insight is worth. But first, you have to know *yourself* what it is worth.

೧೮೨೦

There is always an intention tax: Are you willing to face your issues to move forward? In Paulo Coehlo's *The Alchemist*, the hero's mentor says he needs a tenth of his sheep to help him on his journey. The shepherd spends a pensive evening thinking about the request and, suddenly, realizes that a tenth of his current livelihood is worth fulfilling his destiny. The mentor, adorned in a gold breastplate, says that he didn't really need the sheep. He needed to make sure that the hero was committed to the journey. Not that the mentor knew he was serious, but that the hero *himself* knew he was serious.

When a family member or friend lends you money or other resources, the first question from them is not, "When will you get it back to me?" Even the bank doesn't ask you this first. The first question is, always, "What are you going to do with it?" The universe is the same way. It wants you to commit, then it will open up the doors. You can fill out the forms, you can say how much you want it, and you can sit in bitterness because you don't have it, whether it is the million dollars in the bank, the right job, or fabulous fame, but without knowing how you are going to use it – knowing your "why?" – then the chances of it arriving are as slim as a toothpick. It is intention, not desire, that puts the wheels in motion.

I don't like owing people. It's like a nervous tick that bypasses my thoughts, an automatic reaction. I chose to be an independent creative, and we always owe someone. This is a personal dilemma. We owe our family and friends the time they gave us to work on our craft, and that is time we didn't spend with them. We owe financial commitments, particularly when we first start out, as others have to have flexibility as we discover how to bring in income, and that journey is often an infinite one. We owe ourselves, the indebtedness of the aforementioned time, the opportunity cost of stability, and the weight of believing our trek is worthwhile to ourselves, which is why, if we don't understand why we do what we do, then that weight becomes guilt or shame or hopelessness. We owe, we owe, we owe.

So when I have had lean times, usually marked by a pivot to another world, the investment of, say, previous capital to new ventures, working hard at an old discipline to help fund the new discipline I care about more while phasing it out and seeing the old money come less and less while the new money hasn't quite come yet, then I see myself facing my fear: Asking for support. Could I get latitude on this bill? How can we barter for this necessity? What ways can we get this commitment down to something more managable?

It feels like drowning.

And then I make the first step for support. Then the second. I begin breathing. I realize my ability to function independently is directly tied to my perception of self worth. I'm afraid admitting things are not going how I expected, that I have been hit with the unexpected, that my master plan needs deviation, makes me less of who I am. The cycle of independence and dependence, the wheel of fortune on which we all ride, brings me closer to acceptance.

It's like coming up for air. The lungs get bigger over time. It stops feeling like drowning. And when the current does change again, you'll be prepared.

I ask, "How would it feel if the lost check arrived or if the delinquent client suddenly direct deposited my money. I'd feel a sense of release, as if the birds began singing and everything, and I mean everything, was suddenly right in the world. But real pain doesn't shut off that quickly. It lingers, and leaves slowly, like a swelling going down. That's when I know it's not real pain, but circumstantial pain. It is temporary. That's when I know I'll get through it fine and, a year from now, I will not remember the circumstances of this all-consuming moment, if I remember it at all. I know I was in a financial bind exactly a year ago. I couldn't tell you its face, nevertheless its name.

The opposite is true, too: Just like blurry, scary faces in a nightmare, our own desires remain ethereal until we pin them down. The worst thing you can say is, "If I had a million dollars." It points to two negatives. First, a lack of gratitude for the resources you currently have, the very resources, fortified with luck and grace, that brought you to this point to even have this moment of thought. You aren't maximizing what you've got now, because you don't even consider your current resources worthy of your attention. It's smacking the universe in the face.

Second, you don't achieve your goals with round numbers. To paraphrase the late motivational speaker Jim Rohn, how can you handle $1,000,000 if you don't know what happened to the $5 in your pocket? You need specifics to do great works. If you're going to be rich, then what is your definition of rich? If you need money to get your idea started, then how much do you need and, more importantly, where will each resource go? It is the exact same thing with time, as if you need time to create, then how exactly will you use that time?

My turning point came reading Mike Michalowicz's *Profit First*. He recommends independents and small business owners put their money into buckets – the same, classic grandmotherly concept of putting cash into different envelopes or coffee cans. You get a check and it's automatically split into the predetermined groups. As an independent creative, you may get a big check today… and not get another one for weeks, if not months, and may have a completely different pattern next year, so creating your own system is crucial. It's worth reading for this discussion alone.

But what if you applied that same principle to all your resources? "Where did the time go?" is just as deadly to your career as "If I had a million dollars." I don't know where your time went. It was your time! Those specifics become your currency, not only to yourself, but to others, too. Venture capitalist Arlan Hamilton says she's more likely to trust a single mom with her investment money, as the woman would be adept at maximizing her resources every day. This is the key: You can charge what you want, if you make sure that your customer – the investor, the buyer, the public, whomever – knows that you will give them many times the value. The only way is to know what you're going to do with the extra resources you desire.

Sit down and figure out what you need to achieve. How much does that certification cost? What time would it take to learn how to code? Where are your potential customers and what would it require to meet them? Write it all down. We usually don't need a million dollars, nor do we need a week of solitude to get stuff done. We usually just need a few hundred bucks and 30 minutes a day for the next week. This is both inspiring and terrifying, as you'll realize you already have everything you need and the real block or challenge isn't in your resources, but in your mind.

⋘⋙

The people you owe are not your adversaries. They give you the privilege to do what you do. The car note. The credit card bill. The grocery budget. *The Soul of Money* author Lynne Twist recommends putting "Thank you" on the notes section of your checks, giving the universe a humble nod for allowing you the opportunity to have the thing you are paying for. If you resent paying for and having the responsibility of an economy car and a low-rent apartment, then how can you set yourself up for something more? You can't. You want protection from that resentment, that pain, and in doing so, you block out everything. You're trapping yourself in a cycle, for when you ask for money, price your products, or are asked what you charge for your special gift, then you're going to undercut yourself to stay safe from that resentment, that pain, that burden of living at a higher level than you do now.

You decide what you're worth based on how you accept things as they are now. It doesn't mean you have to be happy with where you are now. It is appreciating what you have within the context of your current life. This isn't a nicety, or a treatise on gratitude or thankfulness. You resent people not paying top dollar for your work, setting the expectation that everyone will pay up to *this* much for your type of work, so when you are setting your price, being asked what something is worth, or sitting at the negotiation table, you are less likely to give a number reflective of what you could and should be getting, and more likely to acquiesce when someone gives you a low ball number because, in your mind, that is just what people do. The only thing you can change, the only thing you need to change, is what you do. The people around you, everything around you, will respond accordingly.

Your worth is like a star. The stars you see in the sky tonight are based on light that's taken a long time to travel, so long, in fact, that some of the stars that you see in the sky have actually burnt out, collapsed, and died years ago. What you are witnessing is an afterglow, the last gasping shadow of a structure. What you are witnessing is the past. So, if you act according to what you see at the moment, then you are building your life based on signals that are no longer accurate. It also means new, budding structures, growing just outside of your point of view, will be decorating your future, but they are happening on a level you can't see just yet. It could be a new client who has been quietly watching you and thinks you can handle a serious job for a serious budget. It could be a great opportunity at the true stature of what you can contribute to the world. It could be a dynamite partner worthy of your current and future potential. And like an external star, bound by the properties of astronomy, your opportunities will react to you based on the bounds of your own internal belief system. A new-to-you client offers a budget ten times what you're current getting, but you offer your services at a fraction of the price and worth based on your own past beliefs. A giant opportunity rolls right up to your doorstep, but you go for the small ideas instead because it enables you to stay comfortable. A collaborator creates a rare chance for you to be pushed, challenged, and motivated to be a better creator, yet you suddenly find many reasons not to move forward. Your reasoning may be sound, maybe even right, but they are right based on the wrong system. They are based on what was, not on what is. They are based on the past. It is us looking intensely at the night sky, searing the visual into our brains, and making decisions based on our old view without ever looking up at the sky again. To move forward, to move closer to your greatness, you simply need to stop for a moment, take a breath, and look at where you truly are. In this case, your potential new opportunities, outside partnerships, and self-generated ideas are your constellations.

People cannot help you on your journey when you don't communicate what you desire and what you deserve. If you're not honest about what you really want, you can't help you on your journey, either.

What you "owe", then, isn't money, time, or sacrifice, but to turn what has been given into something greater in the world. Like alchemy.

It's replacing weight with levity. Weight is the burden, the pressure, and the fear of what lies ahead based on what has happened before. Levity is taking the reality seriously and making the best decision at the moment. One paralyzes you. One enables you.

༺༻

Honor your beautiful commitments, and they are all beautiful. They are your stake in the ground, your anchor of certainty, on which you build your life. They are to be adorned like tapestries and obelisks on which you fashion your foundation. If you listen, they bring the jewels and the surprises. Every day.

The circumstances delivering you pain will eventually receed, through time or through tolerance or through insight, but the wisdom gained will remain, glistening on the shore like seashells. The pain will go away. Do not be angry at the circumstances, or at the situations, or at the luck. You cannot be angry at a particular moment in your life without being ungrateful for the riches it gave you. One cannot exist without the other. They are one in the same.

The Greek and Chinese words for chaos are virtually synonymous with another term: opportunity. We can make the most progress when things are uprooted and previous boundaries blur, It just doesn't feel like it. Our perceived loss requires us to reach higher than before. We now have no past to defend.

The dying are often thankful for the experience of dying. They suddenly have clarity of purpose and firmness of priorities elusive to us during our regular lives. Why? It's not from being afraid or delusional, but being grateful for having life in the first place. I had an unexpected bout with cancer in my early thirties and, in short order, my perspective changed, just as it did a few years later finding out I was going to become a father. They are the same experience: Realizing everything is finite. What is forever? Love is forever. Knowledge is forever.

Your tough time is not forever. Your wisdom will be. If you choose to take it.

Trust the Wheel of Fate, for it is what brought you here.

The chess pieces are **exactly** where they are supposed to be. You would never say that the game was unfair, that it robbed you. You would never throw the game away, flipping the board and starting over again. You would never say that it, or you, were broken. Players do their best when they trust where things lay. Time management expert and long-time jogger Laura Vanderkam says she had no problem committing to running every single day when she stopped asking *if* she was going to run today, but *when* she was going to run today. Same with your life. Throwing fists at the walls of unfairness is a full-time job better spent working within the circumstances, rules, and borderlines in your given life. You're able to soar, because only then you can maximize the resources you have available by having appreciation and gratitude for what you have at hand. Ironically, you have to create love, acceptance, and reverence for where you are at now to change your situation. Lynne Twist put it well: "When we let go of the chase for more, and consciously examine and experience the resources we already have, we discover our resources are deeper than we knew or imagined. In the nourishment of our attention, our assets expand and grow."

The trick is to fully participate in your life, even when your life isn't where you want it to be. It is to be fully present when you don't want to show up that day. It is to be here.

III
SHARE YOUR WORTH
YOU HAVE A LEGACY

"Think of your work life, therefore, not as separate from your spiritual life, but as central to your spiritual life. Whatever your business, it is your ministry. Every relationship, every activity, every circumstance is part of your ministry, to the extent that you think of it that way. Such devotion uplifts the vibration of your thinking, thus improving the experience others have of you and that you have of them... Energy can create wealth, but wealth itself cannot build energy."

Marianne Williamson,
The Law of Divine Compensation

The easiest motivation and the laziest shield from harm is anger. It is also the most treacherous. We're taught to show the world that it can't hold us down. Show them who's boss. I *will* make an impact today and you can't stop me! Best case scenario, one day, you would have shown the world how much of a bad ass you are, and there will be no more battles to fight, no more prizes to win. The most driven people can find themselves miserable in their mansion or their private jet or their worldwide TV show or whatever trinket of personal success. When they get to the so-called top, they realize that they were motivated by winning, which means, by their definition, someone else has to lose. What happens when you do win? Many of us don't think that through. And that vengeful, prove 'em wrong attitude doesn't just dissipate when you achieve what you say you want. It doesn't have a release, so you begin creating adversaries because you need enemies to stay motivated or, worse, subconsciously plot your own downfall so you can have another mountainpeak to reach. *The Big Leap* author Gay

Hendricks calls this an upper-limit problem, meaning you aren't comfortable with your success because you feel like you don't deserve it or you realize your motivation is going away. So you sabotage it. I'm tired of the accomplished entrepreneur, the established politician, or the amazing athlete share their take after a public, avoidable downfall, finally excited with a glint in her eyes, a conviction in her voice, talking about proving all the doubters wrong and loving being the underdog and envisioning herself back on top, when her drive was missing moments before she made the foolhearty decision in the first place. The only person that didn't believe she would stay on top was her.

The original reason you do things goes away, which is why you can't be motivated by anger.

You should be the same to whom you serve no matter what your circumstances. The trials seem frustrating, if not unsermountable, when we begin a new journey. For a while, I believed we were tested by a vengeful god, a tough universe, an omnipresent bootcamp sergent wanting only the strong to survive and have the spoils. It is hard to earn.

I've learned differently now. The treasure is initially denied because we need to learn how to show up even when the rewards feel out of reach, when the tangible rewards are questionable at best, and when we aren't sure there will be a payoff at the end. It isn't a test of your ethics or grit. It is guaranteeing that you discover the real treasure: Serving others to your highest capacity.

Delayed gratification means showing up in a consistant manner, whether fiscally rich or broke, impacting audiences large or tiny, or being a bestseller or a minor seller. I worked on my first major book, *Porn & Pong: How Grand Theft Auto, Tomb Raider & Other Sexy Games Changed Our Culture*, for five years, and remained antsy about getting it out into the public after many rewrites, much agent drama, and different personal challenges, until various veteran writers pulled me aside and said my reward wasn't getting it published. I was *already* experiencing my reward: Creating my first manuscript outside of the scrutiny of the public. No one knew who I was and no one cared. There would only be one first book, and, no matter what the success of the book, I would never experience that solitary practice again. My voice was at its purist. They were right. My effort since has been to get back to that essence, to give you my clearest voice, and to serve you my best expression, regardless of how many copies my books sell. I've written best-sellers and I've written just as many flops. My intention is always the same, though, and I could not promise that the intention would have been the same if my first book had earned a six-figure deal before it was done (it didn't) or if I came from the public spotlight (I didn't).

Your core ideas, those core intentions as a creator, are all built in the struggle, not in the feast.

The biggest danger, then, isn't missing your oppportunity to shine brightly, to create wealth, or to impact the world, but not allowing the life experiences to prepare you to do those very things. The circumstances will come in disguises, cloaked in a frustrating situation, a setback, or an unexpected development. Your life is tailor made to develop the muscles you need to succeed.

◦১৪০০

The universe doesn't want to punish you, which is as preposterous as believing gravity dislikes skydivers or flames hate firefighters. It is just physics, science, and nature. And, the universe knows exactly when to give you what you need, like a flower always blossoming on time. Your gifts are never gone, nor do your efforts die unspoken for within a vacuum. There is a wonderful deluge of opportunities on their way to you, with a proverbial hand holding the pressure-pushing door for the right moment to let go. "Hold on, she hasn't figured out this belief yet. Wait, she has to understand her worth before we give her the riches. Let's pause, because if we give this to her now, she won't have gratitude for the success. Not yet, as she doesn't know why she even desires these amazing things in her life." It is not punishment. It is timing.

We may respect the timing, but we almost certainly do not know *why* the timing. It could be something for us to learn or, potentially more maddening, it could be something that someone else must learn or an environmental change that needs to happen first. Have you ever had a desire that wasn't getting fulfilled and frustrated you to no end, and then circumstances change, you receive what you want, and you notice how it would have been unremarkable, if not impossible for it to happen any other time? When we say, "The timing was perfect.", it's not a parlor trick we pull on ourselves. No, within that **bundle of gratitude** is knowing the event, the thing, the idea appeared just on time – not too early, not too late – like the evening train. That's why gratitude speeds up the journey to your next best life. You are focused on the beauty coming your way, which means you aren't wasting time, energy, or emotion questioning the process.

Energy is more eager to fill an area where a space has already been carved for it. Giving gratitude for your next wonderful opportunity is not just good practice, but makes room for the event to happen. It's not trying to occur in a life that doesn't have space for it to happen. You've been saying this for years without directly saying it: "I began focusing on the wonderful friends, career, and health in my life and, of course, that's when I met my soulmate.", or "I began taking care of my customers instead of trying to make a quick buck, and that's when my business really took off.", and so on. Think about your life. Every example holds complete acceptance and unflinching gratitude, twin emotions that give us joy today and space for beauty tomorrow.

The universe doesn't care if you do "right" or "wrong". It's not testing you. It is confirming you want to behave based on your previously stated thoughts, desires, and intentions. Hypocrisy doesn't stand a chance. This is good news: You are empowered to create your own destiny – and have it supported organically by your environment – by being clear about what you really want in your life. There is a classic computer programming saying: "Garbage in, garbage out". In other words, you build the framework for whatever experience you are having, which is why we are handed some of our toughest battles and, if we survive, we have the indestructible resilience we desired in the first place. If you don't like your settings, then change in which you align.

ഗ≥

Spiritual author Caroline Myss compares our ever-winding success path to hitting road construction. We have a full tank of gas, we got our destination set, and we are eager to arrive. Then detour street signs appear, or perhaps our GPS beeps warning us of upcoming delays, and we realize we have to take a different way. We follow the signs and take the detour. The detour could be for a quick moment, it could be for several miles. It really doesn't matter. We watch the signs and keep an eye on our GPS *until it tells us to get back on the original track*. In the interim, we don't question if Cleveland disappeared. We don't wonder if we deserve to make it to Cleveland. We don't ask if the car is broken, the GPS is wrong, or the signs are incorrect. We just trust the process and know that the original path, now fraught with incomplete bridges, fresh tar, or other hazards, isn't our best way. You don't skip the detour signs and try to cross a broken highway anyway.

Questioning is the source of our grief as well as the source of our insight. The difference is in the questions we ask. "Why isn't this happening yet?" or "Why are they successful and I'm not?" creates a different context than "Why am I on this particular road?" or "How can I make the world better from this viewpoint?" We always choose how much we learn from our circumstances.

The best approach to your goal of career prosperity is to act as if it isn't coming. That doesn't mean it isn't coming. It means if someone says they are going to come at 10:30 a.m., then you're not standing there at 10:29 a.m. with your hand on the doorknob. Trust.

The mistrust doesn't come from not believing that we will reach our destination. That is a misnomer. Our mistrust comes from not believing we deserve to reach the destination. Why should you have the power to influence millions of people? Why should you have enough money to live a comfortable life? The answer, of course, is another question: Why not? Legendary marketer Seth Godin talks about the origin of the word "genius", which initially was used to describe your unique gift to the world, but, about a century ago, became a way to separate "gifted people" from the rest of us. We think we are being humble honoring other people when we call them "geniuses", but are subtly deifying what are just ordinary humans with the same hours of the day. The pain comes from the separation, the thin line between us and them, that shoots down our vision before it even has a chance to come through.

My colleague got a surprise offer to do a new kind of job. They already had a stable, long-time career with another, more traditional organization, and was fine with what it had delivered, but was still intrigued by the new opportunity. It was based on their hard-earned skillset, but still out of their comfort zone. It would be a risk. I recommended having a conversation with the agency the upcoming weekend, but warned that they would forever be changed by the experience. Once you view yourself in an expanded way, which sometimes happens when we listen to how *others* describe us in an expanded way, then it is impossible to go back to your previous view. It is a rubber band that cannot be unstretched. They had the conversation and decided against pursuing it.

Walking into their current job on Monday morning, though, was like going into a totally new organization. They said it was like seeing the truth for the first time. Of course, the organization didn't change overnight. They did. More specifically, their own value of self raised because they heard and accepted that their worth was more than just this one opportunity at this one organization. You can be sure that the organization recognized their shift, too, and treated them with more respect because it knew that *they* knew how valuable they were, and were more eager to make opportunities to show them how much they were valued within the organization.

That's what happens when we see our true worth within the world: Everything seems new. It is like you found the cheat code, or in the climactic *The*

Matrix scene when Neo sees everything for what it truly is underneath the intimidating surface. There is a system in place, and it reacts to how you show up. On better days, I can feel, and almost see, the exchange between you and I, between one and another, as we are contributing to the flow of life, and responding to our declarations, and fulfilling, or not fulfilling, our needs from moment to moment. We are all attached, like some complex, infinite game of Cat's Cradle, with you determining what kind of world you want to live in.

When we believe that we have no impact, we do damage to our potential power, value, and service. As a long-time freelance writer, I connect with people who believe they are a mercinary, a hired gun that churns out hit after hit, and, like a ronin, silently takes his or her reward and moves on to the next proverbial village. There is no sentimentality and, seemingly, no reflection. It is a much easier perspective to have as you juggle the daily needs of the creative business and of your health and of your loved ones and of your personal life. It is safer to feel removed from the rhyme or reason or even impact of your work to focus on a so-called higher order of being a worker. But it just *feels* like you are extracting love from the labor. There is still a reason why you do a particular line of work. You could be an insurance salesman because your dad was one, and even if you hate it, you still are involved because of a love or, at minimum, respect you had for your father and any impressions, however forgotten or repressed, of him while you were young doing that same work that you do today.

I realized my own history just a year ago. I was in Detroit supporting Chris Guillebeau's book *Side Hustle*, and I ended up chatting with a Michigander afterwards. He shared how his whole family had side hustles, but no one called them side hustles – I first heard the term myself in Silicon Valley around 2009. But this guy's family wouldn't say side hustle, but they would say "I know a guy…" or "Talk to Uncle Charlie, he does this thing…". "This thing...", the guy said, ended up helping his family keep food on the table. It wasn't Mafia talk or anything deep, but just relatives who were good with cars or could bake a damn tasty cake and so on. We laughed about how amazing it was, and how perceptive it was of him to realize it. Driving home, I suddenly realized he and I were one in the same: My dad has been an independent cartoonist and publisher since I was a child, my favorite uncle has owned his popular tire shop for decades along with doing a full-scale, mobile carnival ride business during the summer, and my grandfather on another branch of the family owned a series of bars and tire shops from when he was in his twenties until his death in his sixties. His son, my pop that raised me, started his own mortgage business and did quite well until wrapping up after the 2008 housing market colapse. One random day, I remember coming home from high school and seeing my pop beaming about a big check he received. He was proud, and he wanted me to be proud of him, too, though, as a teen, I could only understand so much.

I didn't know, or couldn't concieve the work that went into that five-figure check, or that things were tight just the week before, or that he may have thought about giving up on that very deal, or on the business itself, when things suddenly came together.

But I understand now.

Not one of my African-American predecessors called themselves an entrepreneur. I don't recall ever hearing it come out of my family's mouth. Back then the word was still French, as in used primarily in France. And yet, it planted seeds in me, watching each and every one struggle and beam and fight and declare themselves, through action and persistance and vision, saying "I'm here to make my mark", These ideas, like me knowing what to charge the market for my services, or being able to negotiate based on some seemingly invisible service I provide, or even me knowing the value of what I bring to a world that isn't ready for it today, but will be ready for it tomorrow, I do not and cannot take full credit for that. I watched them, just like you watched others. But it was up to me to toil that soil, and that process begins with even recognizing that the seeds are there.

This is why you cheat yourself when you don't connect the dots. There is always a pattern. You may not even like the pattern, and that's ok, for you can change the pattern of your future, and no time, no matter how frustrating, is wasted time. And often, without that previous time, you wouldn't have came to this moment when you realize what you must do next. There is no one without the other.

When did you start this path? When was the first time you were paid to do what you do to pay you bills? Start at the beginning. Dig out the contract, if you have it, and see how they describe you, and how you describe your services. Is this you? Is this still you? As I said in *The Ultimate Bite-Sized Entrepreneur*, if you haven't created a new baseline for your market value, what you're worth, and how you serve in five years, then you are making decisions based on who you were five years ago. Picture my Kindergarten child holding the same values as an infant, or your 30-year-old self making the same choices as your 25-year-old self. It is ridiculous, at best. And yet, we create these magnificent, epic careers doing our thing, and do not take the time to actually see why we're doing this thing, how we are being valued for doing this thing, and what we're contributing by continually doing this thing.

Your monetary lack is a direct reflection of you not knowing the purpose. "To put food on the table" is a purpose, but that doesn't prevent you from spending 15 minutes a day working on a side hustle you really care about, or watching a YouTube video that will educate you on making your big idea a reality. But all that is unhelpful until you actually get still enough, you stop enough, you value your life enough to reflect on what you really want. To paraphrase *Pivot* author Jenny Blake, you can have the joy and the money. I would add, though, you first have to know what brings you joy. These dots, from your family, from your childhood, from your career thus far, clue you in on what brings you joy. There is a reason why you do the work you do – otherwise, you wouldn't be doing it.

Poet Mark Nepo says when we immerse ourselves into our craft, then, for that moment, we are connected to everyone else who has ever done it before. How honorable is that? You are not a struggling artist, but someone participating in the same actions, and perhaps facing the same feelings, as Michaelangelo and Picasso and O'Keefe. By doing what you are called to do, by doing what you do best, by doing what only you can do in your special way, then you are not just honoring yourself, but you are honoring those that came before you and the sacrifices they made to make your profession even valid. Edison is equal to Jobs is equal to you. This is your ancestry. They have probably felt the pain you feel now. They probably conquered it, too. That means you can as well.

It means that bringing your true power, value, and service to the table is up to you. To paraphrase James Baldwin, your crown has already been bought and paid for – often in blood. Isn't it time you wore it?

Conclusion
Become your own patron

"Failure has a function: It asks you if you really want to go on making things."

Elizabeth Gilbert,
Big Magic

Well before becoming an author, or even an adult, I spent years studying isoteric histories. I was fascinated by astrology and astronomy, Tarot and crystal balls, and Jungian arguments and Hero's Journey theories. People often described me as a laidback, light-hearted kid, but internally I was, and still am, fascinated by the shadow, the parts that we don't know of ourselves. As a late teen, *The Complete Jung* and the *Classical Mythology* textbook were regular, comfort reading.

In one non-fiction book, I read about highly-spiritual monks investigating potentially dangerous religious areas. It may have been a temple thought cursed by a dark entity, or a church that needed to be blessed by a grounded, focused force like themselves.

The monks, however powerful, never go it alone, though.

Instead, one brave monk leads the group into the dangerous area. The other members begin tying a rope tightly around the waist of the leader and then, ever so carefully, cinching their hands around the lagging rope and bracing themselves as the leader opened the door. They remain outside as the brave monk goes inside.

The theory is this: If things get out of hand, then the group pulls the lead monk back to safety. He had an out. And the monk felt more free to explore, as he knew he could be pulled out of a jam.

He relaxed.

From my reading, this is why certain monk sects to this day still wear frayed ropes around their cloth. It's not just practical to keep their loincloth intact, but a subtle reminder that they are always protected by the group. They are never lost. They are alone, but never abandoned.

☙❧

As I'm finishing this book, on New Year's Eve 2018, I feel the weight, not the levity, of my progress. The pieces don't feel like they are coming together or, more accurately, the parts are not coming together as quickly as I want or need them to be. It is one thing to not be sure what needs to be done. It is quite another to not be sure if you have the capacity to make the journey.

It is in these moment you have to become your own energy source. No one cares about your particular mission, desire, or impact as much as you do. Recently, an entrepreneur confessed her frustration not finding employees as passionate as she was about her business. She will probably always be frustrated, as she will never find someone as passionate as she is – otherwise, they'd be starting their own business. Your momma, your partner, and your advocates hopefully have your back. You need to man the front.

Moments like my New Year's Eve will always happen to you. They remind you that you are the ancient monk, in your new, dangerous, highly spiritual place, and you are alone. You are always alone.

Your safety rope is your own awareness.

Sometimes others won't treat you at your true worth, often because they are holding more financial or veto power and abusing the imbalance. You need to build great partnerships not just based on the needs of the money or of the ego, but on how positive you feel working with the other. That positive feeling will naturally create creative, emotional, and potentially financial prosperity. Everything starts with a feeling. The energy from the feeling opens up the new opportunities.

Sometimes the ends will not meet. The resources you get from a beautifully-done endeavor may be a great contact for future ideas, a cool story to tell people later, or a brilliant vision of what could be next for you. In the meantime, get your bread. There is no shame in that. I love Elizabeth Gilbert's take, in *Big Magic*, about keeping a day job for years after becoming a professional writer, saying "I was always willing to work hard so my creativity could play lightly, and, in so doing, I became my own patron."

And sometimes, the world won't seem to see your purpose. The worst way to create is to say you want your thing to be embraced by the world. It is too earnest. You open the door to grandstanding and preaching. And what if your thing isn't embraced by the world? The bitterness will leach from your skin, and others will probably sense your resistance even before you give them the thing, as they recognize it in you when you share the idea and they don't have an immediately positive reaction. Instead of being embraced by the world, how do you want to transform one person? Literally, just one. Make the goal of serving one and, when you do make an impact, your appreciation will shine and nourish you when you have those dark, cold nights.

All successes are based on quantum leaps, be it having a fabulous business partnership, a highly profitable business, or a true appreciation by the world. It isn't there, then it is. You don't know when the switch will flip. As Deepak Chopra says, "When and where will bubbles appear in a pot of boiling water?" It is binary, and sudden, and unpredictable. We know that it *will* happen, though, providing we keep the pot on a consistant source.

Understanding your creative power, value, and service is your consistant source, your monk's rope, your allies on this journey. It is the ouroboros, the mythological snake eating its own tail. It is nourished forever. Imagine never retiring, not because you need to work to live, but because you live to work. You live to serve. You feed it, and then it feeds you. Forever.

Your job, then, isn't to predict the leap to success, nor to wait for success before you begin. Your job is to serve, and in serving, your true worth will always come to you.

It begins when you bring your worth to the table.

It begins with you.

Let's Connect!

This book is just the beginning of your growth. Here's how we keep the conversation going.

Get Bonus Content & More
http://www.JoinDamon.me

Get your free business worth toolkit to gain even more insight into your next steps. You'll also get exclusive content, early previews of new goodies, and a weekly discussion with fellow creators!

One-on-One Guidance
http://www.damonbrown.net

I'd love to help you organize your priorities, apply THE BITE-SIZED ENTREPRENEUR method, and make room for your best career. We can set up a time to chat and see if we're a good fit. Reach out at damon@damonbrown.net.

Do the Bite-Sized Entrepreneur Boot Camp
http://www.bsbootcamp.com

This six-part, self-guided course will bring the best out of your current productivity, focus, and creativity. Taking the book series a step further, THE BITE-SIZED ENTREPRENEUR boot camp is perfect to do at your own pace with my guidance through video, audio, and text. Join through JoinDamon.me to get a special discount on and one-on-one coaching opportunities!

SPEAKING AT YOUR EVENT
http://www.damonbrown.net

I am happy to talk about your event and how a discussion on mindfulness, productivity, or entrepreneurship can best fit your needs. International venues are welcome, as are American events, and my platforms include TED, Colombia 4.0 in Bogota, and American University in Washington D.C. My keynote talks are also available and discussed in detail on the next section, **AVAILABLE KEYNOTE TALKS**.

AVAILABLE KEYNOTE TALKS

Damon is available to speak worldwide at select events, conferences, and companies. His audiences have included the main TED Conference, second stage, in British Columbia, American Underground tech incubator in Durham, NC, Colombia 4.0 in Bogota, Colombia, the Adult Entertainment Expo in Las Vegas, and American University in Washington D.C. Damon's talks interweave personal narrative and industry knowledge with actionable strategies. He is also happy to include Q & As and panel discussion as well as moderating panels and interviewing other leaders.

Watch Damon's speakers reel at http://bit.ly/DamonTalks.
Contact: damon@damonbrown.net.

PROFIT
HOW TO CREATE YOUR TRUE WORTH

Creatives often undervalue their services to the market, to their bank account, and to the world. In this inspiration and practical talk, Damon shares the best ways we can joyfully make a living off our craft, create business partnerships worthy of our skills, and truly be of service to others.

PRODUCTIVITY
THE POWER OF GOOD ENOUGH

What is the number one killer of innovation? Perfection. With perfection, the key motivation often isn't having high standards, but being afraid of making a mistake. In this talk, I share the three powerful strengths you get when you let perfection go.

ENTREPRENEURSHIP
WHY YOU CAN (AND SHOULD) START YOUR SIDE HUSTLE IMMEDIATELY

Believe it or not, we already possess most of the skills we need to create our passion-driven business. So why aren't most people pursuing their potentially profitable ideas? They are intimidated by the small gap in their skill set. In this immediately actionable talk, Damon shares how to easily traverse that gap and explains the three crucial strengths every successful entrepreneur possesses. This talk inspires both potential entrepreneurs and ambitious upstarts.

SIGNIFICANT REFERENCES

- Esther & Jerry Hicks. *The Vortex: Where the Law of Attraction Assembles All Cooperative Relationships* (Hay House 2009).

- Steven Pressfield. *The Author's Journey: The Wake of the Hero's Journey and the Lifelong Pursuit of Meaning* (Black Irish Entertainment 2018).

- Brene Brown. *Braving the Wilderness: The Quest for True Belonging and the Courage to Stand Alone* (Random House 2017).

- Elizabeth Gilbert. *Big Magic: Creative Living Beyond Fear* (Riverhead Books 2015).

- Caroline Myss. *Sacred Contracts: Awakening Your Divine Potential* (Harmony 2001).

- Deepak Chopra. *The Spontaneous Fulfillment of Desire: Harnessing the Infinite Power of Coincidence to Create Miracles* (Harmony 2003).

- Mike Michalowicz. *Profit First: Transform Your Business from a Cash-Eating Monster to a Money-Making Machine* (Portfolio 2017).

- Mark Nepo: 7,000 Ways to Listen. *Oprah's Super Soul Conversations.* December 2018.

- Jenny Blake: How to Optimize for Revenue and Joy. *The Pivot podcast.* October 2015.

- Gay Hendricks. *The Big Leap: Conquer Your Hidden Fear and Take Life to the Next Level*

(HarperOne 2009).

- Paulo Coehlo. *The Alchemist* (HarperOne 1989)
- Srinivas Rao. *Unmistakable: Why Only is Better than Best* (Portfolio 2016)
- Laura Vanderkam. *Off the Clock: Feel Less Busy While Getting More Done* (Portfolio 2018)
- Marianne Williamson. *The Law of Divine Compensation: On Work, Money, and Miracles* (HarperOne 2012).

Acknowledgements

Thank you to the masters: Esther, Jerry and Abraham Hicks, Caroline Myss, Les Brown, Brene Brown, Chase Jarvis, Seth Godin, Deepak Chopra, Mike Michalowicz, Mark Nepo, Gay Hendricks, and Lynne Twist as well as my personal colleagues Laura Vanderkam, Jenny Blake, Nilofer Merchant, Srinivas Rao, Arlan Hamilton, Alex Goetz, Jeanette Hurt, and Bec Loss. Hat tip to Will Lucas, Monique Woodard, Jason Kucsma, Deborah Blumberg, Susan Johnston Taylor, Sherri Beck Paprocki, Charmaine Houck, Kim Nagy, Hilary Sutton, Priest Willis, Cynthia Kosciuczyk, and Dan Kaplan for the support.

A nod to Sade's *Promise*, Travis Scott's *Astroworld*, Pusha T's *Daytona*, and Peter Allen's *Taught By Experts* for providing the writing soundtrack and Purple Fluorite for providing the excellent audiobook music.

And love to Bernadette Johnson, Tony Howard,

David G. Brown, A. Raymond Johnson, and Deirdra Bishop, and to Parul Patel and Alec and Abhi Brown.

About the Author

Damon Brown is a long-time journalist and author of several books, most notably the best-selling *The Ultimate Bite-Sized Entrepreneur Trilogy* (2017) and *Porn & Pong: How Grand Theft Auto, Tomb Raider and Other Sexy Games Changed Our Culture* (Feral House 2008), as well as the coffeetable book *Playboy's Greatest Covers* (Sterling Publishing 2012). BRING YOUR WORTH is his 24th book.

Damon co-founded the social meetup app Cuddlr while being the primary caretaker to his infant son. It went number one on the Apple App store twice, changing the cultural conversation around platonic intimacy. The app was acquired less than a year after it launched, and the whirlwind experience inspired Damon's popular *Inc.com* column Sane Success as well as THE ULTIMATE BITE-SIZED ENTREPRENEUR. Since the Cuddlr acquisition, Damon has coached hundreds of non-traditional entrepreneurs. In 2019, he served as the first

Entrepreneur-in-Residence at the Toledo Library.

You can catch Damon in *Playboy*, *Fast Company*, and *Entrepreneur*, as well as at any locale that serves really spicy food. He lives in Las Vegas, Nevada, with his wife, two young sons, and bottles of hot sauce.

Connect with him at www.JoinDamon.me or on Twitter at @browndamon.

www.ingramcontent.com/pod-product-compliance
Lightning Source LLC
Chambersburg PA
CBHW071746240526
45471CB00022B/592